SPECIAL

COOKBOOK

MARY
PATTERSON

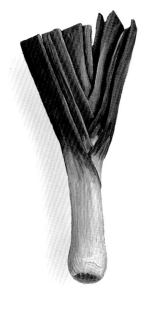

IMAGES BY
SHAWN SHEPHERD

POLYCHROME FINE ARTS & PUBLISHING CO.

Patterson, Mary
SPECIAL COOKBOOK

Shepherd, Shawn
Illustrations

Printed in China by Everbest Printing Company Ltd.

Designed and published by
Polychrome Fine Arts & Publishing Co.
Victoria   British Columbia   Canada
2007

ISBN 978-0-9780210-1-6

POLYCHROME FINE ARTS & PUBLISHING CO.
www.polychromefinearts.com

FOR MY PARENTS

SPECIAL CONTENTS

A good apple is better than an insipid peach.

Leigh Hunt, *The Examiner*

In Denmark, Sweden and the U.S., a polished apple is a traditional gift for a teacher. This practice stemmed from the fact that teachers during the 16th, 17th and 18th centuries were poorly paid. Parents would compensate the teacher by providing food. As time went on and teachers' pay increased, donations of apples reduced from bushels to single apples.

JONAGOLD RINGS, PORK SCALOPPINE AND DIJON

A comforting autumn dish, using apples straight from the harvest when they are at their best.

serves 4

1 pound pork tenderloin, trimmed of silverskin, cut across the grain into 1-inch pieces then pounded into 3/4-inch thick scaloppine with the side of a chef's knife
salt and pepper
2 tablespoons olive oil
1 tablespoon unsalted butter
3 tablespoons minced shallots
1 Jonagold apples (or Granny Smith) peeled, cored and cut into 12 rings
1/3 cup apple cider vinegar
3 tablespoons calvados
1/2 cup chicken stock
1/4 cup crème fraîche or whipping cream
2 tablespoons Dijon

1 In a large heavy-bottomed fry pan, sauté the pork scaloppine in the olive oil, in batches of six. Sear to brown, 1 1/2 minutes per side until firm to the touch. Transfer to a plate, reserving the pan juices.

2 Heat the butter in the scaloppine pan. Sauté the shallots and apple rings until the apple rings caramelize. Flambé with the calvados. Set the apple and shallot mixture aside. Add the cider vinegar to the pan and reduce to a glaze. Add the chicken stock and reduce by half, add the crème fraîche and reduce by half again. Swirl in the Dijon. Return the apple rings and scaloppine with their juices to the pan and heat through.

3 Divide the scaloppine between 4 plates and serve with a scattering of apple rings.

Accompany
Celeriac purée.

Cooking apples with meats offsets the fattiness of the recipe.

CRÈME BRÛLÉE À LA NORMANDE

Normandy has a reputation for dairy, apples and Calvados. All three ingredients appear in this luxurious dessert.

serves 6

2 cups whipping cream
1/4 cup milk
5 egg yolks
1/3 cup sugar
4 Gala apples (or Granny Smith), peeled, cored and roughly chopped
2 tablespoons unsalted butter
3 tablespoons sugar
2 tablespoons Calvados
6 tablespoons sugar

1 Heat the whipping cream and milk to a bare simmer in a saucepan. Whisk together the yolks with the 1/3 cup sugar in a large bowl, then gradually stir in the whipping cream element. Stirring will ensure that the custard doesn't foam.

2 Sauté the apple slices in the butter for 3 minutes. Add the 3 tablespoons of sugar and cook until the apples are translucent. Flambé with the calvados.

Preheat oven to 300 degrees

3 Distribute the caramelized apple mixture between 6 ramekins and fill the dishes to just over their lip line with the custard. Bake in a bain marie for 45 minutes until set. Refrigerate at least 12 hours.

4 Sprinkle the tops of the custards liberally with sugar and either burn with a torch or under the broiler.

It can be tricky to know when crème brûlées are set. One of my former chefs' tests was to give the ramekins a little shake while the custards were still in the bain marie to see if they were "wobbly all over".

GOLDEN CREAM AND APPLE TART

The custard in this tart soufflés over the apples and does indeed become golden.

serves 6

For the pâte brisée tart shell

1 1/4 cups flour
1/2 teaspoon salt
1 tablespoon sugar
7 tablespoons very cold unsalted butter, in pieces
4 to 5 tablespoons ice water

For the custard filling

3 beaten egg yolks
3/4 cup crème fraîche or whipping cream
3 tablespoons sugar
4 peeled, cored and quartered Granny Smith apples

1 To make the pâte brisée, combine the sifted dry ingredients and cut in the butter until the mixture resembles coarse crumbs. Add the ice water gradually, working the dough into a disc. Chill the dough 1 hour.

2 Roll out the chilled dough into a 12-inch circle. Fit into the 8-inch fluted tart shell, leaving 1 inch of overhang. Press the dough into the pan and tuck the overhanging excess dough to the inside of the tart pan. Chill for 30 minutes.

Preheat oven to 375 degrees

3 Press foil into the chilled tart shell and fill with dried beans or rice to weight the pastry while it's in the oven. Bake until the dough is set and lightly browned, 25 to 30 minutes. Remove the weights and cool.

Set oven to 350 degrees

4 Whisk together the yolks, crème fraîche and 1 tablespoon of the sugar. Fan the apples onto the prepared tart shell, cover with the custard and sprinkle with the remaining 2 tablespoons of sugar. Bake very brown, about 45 minutes. Serve warm.

Choose firm apples with less water content for recipes with exposed apples.

I stick to asparagus which seems to inspire gentle thought.

Charles Lamb, English Essayist

Asparagus is filled with sulphur-containing amino acids that break down during digestion into six sulfur-containing compounds. These can impart a unique smell to urine as they are excreted. Scientists remain divided on why people have different urinary responses to eating asparagus. One camp thinks only about half of the population have a gene enabling them to break down the sulphurous amino acids in asparagus into their smellier components. Others think that everyone digests asparagus in the same way, but only half of us have the gene that enables us to smell the specific compounds formed in the digestion of asparagus.

Asparagus and Mushroom Crêpe Cake

This dish is both extravagant and old world. Well worth the effort for a special meal.

serves 8

For the crêpes

3/4 cup cold water
3/4 cup milk
3 eggs
1 teaspoon salt
1 1/2 cups flour
3 tablespoons melted unsalted butter
2 tablespoons 1/4-inch chive pieces

For the mornay sauce

4 tablespoons flour
4 tablespoons unsalted butter
2 3/4 cups boiling milk
salt and pepper
1/4 teaspoon nutmeg
1/4 cup cream
1 cup grated Swiss cheese

For the asparagus filling

1 tablespoon minced shallots
2 tablespoons unsalted butter
2 ounces chopped, blanched spinach
1 pound steamed chinoise of asparagus
salt and pepper
1 cup mornay sauce

For the mushroom filling

2 cups roughly chopped mushrooms
1 tablespoon minced shallots
2 tablespoons unsalted butter
1 cup ricotta
salt and pepper
1 beaten egg

1 For the crêpes, combine the water, milk, egg and salt in a blender. Pulse, then add the flour and butter, blending for 1 minute. Fold in the chive pieces. Refrigerate at least 2 hours. The batter should just coat the back of a wooden spoon. Add extra water carefully to thin if necessary. Brush a heavy-bottomed 7-inch fry pan with oil and bring it to smoke point. Run a 1/4 cup of batter around the pan and after 1 minute flip and continue cooking the other side of the crêpe for 30 seconds. The crêpes should be very lightly browned. You will have 12 crêpes.

2 For the mornay sauce, melt the butter, add the flour and blend to form a roux, cook 2 minutes. Whisking, add the milk and thicken, 1 minute. Season with the salt, pepper and nutmeg. Add the whipping cream and Swiss cheese. The mixture should coat a spoon well.

3 For the asparagus filling, sauté the shallots in butter until translucent. Off heat, add the spinach, asparagus, salt, pepper and 1 cup of the mornay sauce. Set the mixture aside.

4 For the mushroom filling, sauté the mushrooms in the butter until browned, add the shallots and sauté briefly. Off heat, add the ricotta, salt, pepper and egg. Set the mixture aside.

Assembly

Preheat oven to 350 degrees

5 Butter a 9-inch baking dish, centre a crêpe and spread it with a layer of asparagus filling. Press a crêpe on top and spread it with a layer of mushroom filling. Continue with alternating layers of crêpes and filling, ending with a crêpe. Cover the cake with the remaining mornay sauce. Enclose in foil and bake 1 hour.

6 Serve with a fresh tomato sauce.

Trim asparagus by snapping off the stalks at their natural break point, separating the tender stalks from the wooden end. Peel the stalks of thicker asparagus.

CLASSIC ASPARAGUS VINAIGRETTE

An ideal starter to bring in the local spring harvest.

serves 4

2 egg yolks at room temperature
2 teaspoons Dijon
1 teaspoon white wine vinegar
1 teaspoon lemon juice
5 tablespoons vegetable oil
salt and pepper
40 trimmed asparagus spears
4 teaspoons minced shallots
4 tablespoons finely chopped roasted red peppers
2 tablespoons chopped chervil

1 For the vinaigrette, whisk the yolks and Dijon together. Gradually add the oil, whisking in the vinegar and lemon juice, and season.

2 Blanch the asparagus in boiling salted water until the spears are bright green. Refresh the spears in ice water and pat dry.

Assembly
Divide the asparagus between 4 salad plates, drizzle with the vinaigrette and compose the remaining ingredients around the asparagus.

Asparagus should be eaten quickly after being picked. The spears' natural sugar will turn to starch if left in the refrigerator for more than a few days, leaving the vegetable with less flavour and a woody texture.

ASPARAGUS AND POLENTA WITH POACHED EGGS AND BROWN BUTTER

I was served this dish at a good Italian restaurant in Victoria. One of the chefs made it for his own lunch and found the dish so delicious that it made the menu.

serves 4

4 cups chicken stock
1 cup stone ground cornmeal
1 teaspoon salt
2 tablespoons unsalted butter

4 poached eggs
20 trimmed, blanched asparagus spears
4 tablespoons brown butter *
2 tablespoons chopped parsley

1 For the polenta, bring the stock to a boil in a large heavy-bottomed saucepan, gradually whisk in the cornmeal. Reduce the heat to low and continue to cook until a wooden spoon stands straight up in the polenta. Stir in the salt and the butter into the polenta.

Preheat in oven to 350 degrees

2 Bake the polenta for 20 minutes in a buttered 8x8 inch pan, cool slightly then punch out four 4-inch rounds of polenta.

3 Prepare the eggs, asparagus and brown butter to be ready to join the polenta on the lunch plates.

Assembly
Stack the components of the dish in 4 large shallow bowls as follows: polenta, asparagus and poached eggs to top. Drizzle with the brown butter and shower with parsley.

* Brown butter will give your dishes a delicious nutty flavour. The key to making it is to allow unsalted butter to melt over moderate heat. Swirl the pan once in awhile so that the butter will color evenly. Remove the pan from the heat when the butter is a nut-brown color.

What peaches and what penumbras!
Whole families shopping at night!
Aisles full of husbands!
Wives in the avocados,
babies in the tomatoes!
- and you Garcia Lorca
what were you doing
down by the watermelons?

Allen Ginsberg, *A Supermarket in California*

It is Rudolph Haas we have to thank for the HAAS variety of avocado, the only variety grown year round. The mother tree, to which every Haas avocado tree can be traced, died of root rot at La Habra Heights, California in 2003 at 76 years old. It was chopped down in September of that year and lies lifeless in a Ventura nursery while officials try to figure out what to do with it.

Avocado Grand Duc

Sharing avocados with other mild-flavoured ingredients keeps the buttery texture and faintly nutlike character of the fruit from disappearing.

serves 4

12 ounces hand-peeled shrimp
4 tablespoons mayonnaise
1 tablespoon cocktail sauce
1 teaspoon lemon juice
salt and pepper
2 halved and pitted avocados
2 chopped hardboiled eggs
1 teaspoon chopped fresh tarragon
1 teaspoon chopped fresh parsley
1 teaspoon chopped fresh chervil
4 teaspoons lumpfish caviar

1 Combine the shrimp, mayonnaise, cocktail sauce and lemon juice, and season.

2 Trim the bottom off of each avocado half so they will sit up on a plate and stuff with the shrimp mixture.

3 Arrange the avocados on wide-lipped dishes and garnish with the herbs, chopped egg and caviar.

Lumpfish caviar is dyed red and will run unless used at the last moment.

Avocado with Crispy Bacon

Salty, crispy and creamy all in one appetizing package.

serves 4

1/4 pound bacon rashers, 1/4-inch thick cut
2 tablespoons red wine vinegar
1 tablespoon olive oil
2 teaspoons Dijon
2 avocados
2 tomatoes, peeled, seeded and finely chopped
2 tablespoons chopped basil

1 Chop the bacon into 1-inch pieces and fry till crisp. Pour off the fat and add the olive oil, Dijon and vinegar to the pan. Sauté the bacon in the vinaigrette to heat through.

2 Fan thick wedges of avocado on 4 plates and divide the bacon between them. Garnish with the chopped tomato and basil.

To easily remove an avocado stone with minimum damage to the fruit, cut avocado in half. Jab the stone with the blade of a paring knife and twist it out.

PAN-ROASTED CHICKEN WITH AVOCADO & PAPAYA

Pan-roasting and brining chicken yields a juicy interior and crunchy skin.

serves 4

4 boneless, skin-on chicken breasts
1/2 cup salt
1 tablespoon olive oil
1 tablespoon minced shallots
1/2 cup dry vermouth
3/4 cup chicken stock
3 tablespoons cold butter, in pieces
2 cups roughly chopped avocado
2 cups roughly chopped papaya
salt and pepper

1 Brine the chicken by dissolving the 1/2 cup of salt in 8 cups of water. Refrigerate 30 minutes. Rinse the poultry, pat dry and season with pepper.

Preheat oven to 450 degrees

2 Heat the oil to smoke-point in a heavy-bottomed fry pan. Brown the chicken skin side down for 5 minutes, turn, and cook another 5. Place the fry pan in the oven 10 minutes and bake until the juices run clear. Remove the chicken from the pan and keep warm loosely wrapped in foil.

3 Pour off all but 1 tablespoon of fat from the pan. Sauté the shallots to soften and flambé with the vermouth. When the fire is out, add the stock and simmer rapidly to reduce and thicken the sauce for 6 minutes. Whisk in the butter, incorporate the fruits just to warm and season.

4 Arrange the chicken over the sauce and serve with linguine.

Cook the avocados no longer than a few minutes. Any longer will diminish their delicate flavour.

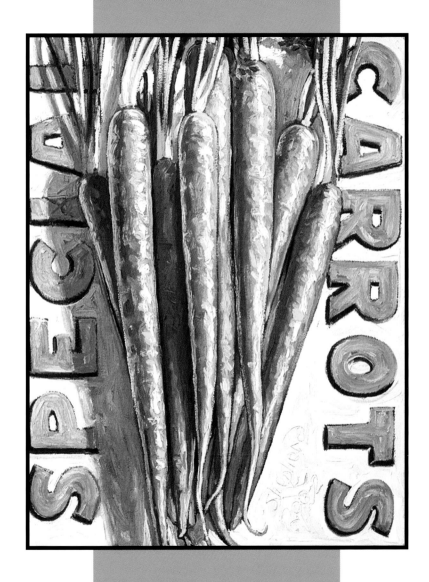

Large, naked, raw carrots are acceptable as food only to those who live in hutches eagerly awaiting Easter.

Fran Lebowitz, *Metropolitan Life*

A diet including plenty of carrots has been touted for years for its efficiency in improving eyesight. The claim is untrue, although carrots are high in vitamin A. During World War 2, Britian's Air Ministry spread the word that eating carrots helped pilots see Nazi bombers attacking at night. The untruth was intended to cover the real matter of what was underpinning the Royal Air Force's successes: Airborne Interception Radar. The secret new system pinpointed some enemy bombers before they reached the English Channel. The disinformation was so persuasive that the English public took to eating carrots to help them find their way to blackout stations. The myth persists at family dinner tables to this day.

CARROT TAPENADE

A baguette spread designed to rival the classic olive version.

makes 1 cup

6 medium peeled, roughly chopped carrots
1 teaspoon roughly chopped garlic
1 tablespoon lemon juice
2 tablespoons olive oil
salt and pepper
2 tablespoons chopped cilantro
1 tablespoon black sesame seeds
cilantro sprigs

1 Steam the carrots until quite tender for 10 minutes and cool slightly. Combine with the garlic, lemon juice and olive oil. Purée the mixture, leaving some texture present. Fold in the cilantro and season. Garnish with black sesame seeds and cilantro sprigs.

2 Serve warm or cold with toasted baguette slices.

If preparing this tapenade in antiquity, the spread would have been purple, the original colour of carrots.

BRAISED CARROTS, FENNEL AND SNOW PEAS

The slight anise flavour and crunch of fennel makes this side dish a good accompaniment to a main course such as a cheese soufflé.

serves 4

1/4 pound snow peas
2 tablespoons olive oil
4 medium carrots, coined
3 trimmed fennel bulbs, in 1/4 inch wedges
1/2 cup chicken stock
salt and pepper
2 tablespoons chopped parsley

1 Steam the snow peas bright green, refresh in ice water, pat dry and reserve.

2 Heat the oil and sauté the fennel and carrots for 3 minutes. Add the stock and simmer covered until the vegetables are tender, 10 minutes. Remove the carrots and fennel and reduce the cooking liquid to thicken. Return all the vegetables to the pan, season and toss with the chopped parsley.

Select young and tender carrots for their fresh green tops, but remove the carrot tops as soon as possible. The greens will rob the roots of moisture and vitamins.

CARROTS AND LENTILS WITH SMOKED BACON

French lentils hold their shape nicely. Salt them during the cooking process to expand their earthy flavour.

serves 6

1/4 pound smoked bacon, in 1/4-inch pieces
2 tablespoons chopped shallots
1 cup rinsed French lentils
3 cups beef stock
1/2 cup full-bodied red wine
1/2 teaspoon salt
3 medium carrots, finely chopped
1 teaspoon chopped fresh thyme
salt and pepper

1 Sauté the bacon until crisp. Pour off all but 1 tablespoon of fat, add the shallots and sauté to soften. Add the lentils, stock, wine and 1/2 teaspoon of salt. Bring the mixture to a boil, then simmer covered for 30 to 45 minutes until the lentils are tender. Add the carrots and cook for another 15 to 20 minutes until they are tender.

2 Season and toss with the chopped thyme.

Accompany
Serve as a bed for veal shanks.

Avoid storing carrots near apples. They emit ethylene gas which can give carrots a bitter taste.

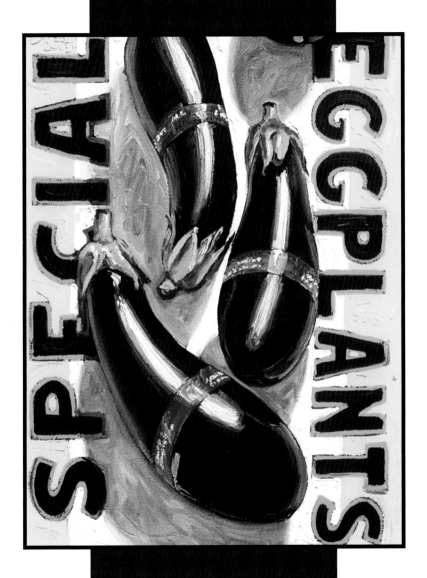

When I was alone, I lived on eggplant, the stove top cook's strongest ally...

Laurie Colwin, *Alone in the Kitchen with Eggplant*

The most famous eggplant dish, eaten all over the Arab world, is called *Imam bayildi,* ' the priest fainted'. This consists of eggplants stuffed with onions and cooked in olive oil. There are two stories about the origin of the name. One is that the priest fainted due to the deliciousness of the dish; the other that he fainted when he learned how much oil was used to cook the dish.

Eggplant caviar

Wealthy folks heap real caviar on toast points. We like eggplant caviar on pita.

makes 3 cups

2 globe eggplants, pierced
6 tablespoons olive oil
2 peeled, seeded and chopped tomatoes
3 tablespoons finely chopped red onion
2 teaspoons minced garlic
1/4 cup chopped basil
2 tablespoons lemon juice
salt and pepper

Green olives and lemon side dish

1 seeded, segmented lemon
2 tablespoons lemon juice
12 large green olives
1 tablespoon parsley
1 pinch saffron, infused in 1 tablespoon warm water
6 tablespoons olive oil
5 tablespoons chopped scallions
salt and pepper

Preheat oven to 350 degrees

1 Slice the eggplants in half by length and brush with 2 tablespoons of olive oil. Lay face down on parchment paper and roast until tender, 30 minutes. Cool, skin and mince, saving the juices.

2 Combine with the remaining ingredients including the remaining 4 tablespoons olive oil, reserved juices and lemon juice. Season and chill until ready to use.

Accompany
For the green olives and lemon side dish, combine the ingredients and rest several hours in the refrigerator to blend the flavours. Serve at room temperature.

Eggplants have a dimple at the blossom end of the fruit. The dimple can be round or oval in shape. The round ones have more seeds and tend to be less meaty.

Roasted eggplant and chèvre terrine

I designed this round terrine to employ surplus eggplants,
zucchinis and bell peppers, which would otherwise have
been out of work.

serves 8

2 pounds eggplants
3 pounds zucchinis
2 tablespoons olive oil
4 pounds mixed red and orange peppers
3 tablespoons basil pesto
4 ounces chèvre
salt and pepper
one 8-inch springform pan
one 7 1/2-inch springform pan bottom

Preheat oven to 400 degrees

1 Split the eggplants and zucchinis by length into 1/4-inch slices and toss in the olive oil, and roast 20 to 30 minutes. Halve the peppers and remove the seeds. Place them skin side up under the broiler. Broil 3 inches from the heat until their skins blacken. Transfer the peppers to a bowl covered with plastic wrap to steam off their skins for 15 to 20 minutes. Remove the skins and season the vegetables.

2 Line the 8-inch springform pan with plastic wrap, letting the wrap overhang the edges of the pan. Layer the roasted vegetables, beginning with half the peppers, laid in a fan pattern alternating, red, orange, red, orange. Distribute 1 tablespoon of pesto over the peppers and continue with layers of zucchini, pesto, eggplant, a centre of chèvre, zucchini, eggplant, pesto and finally a fan pattern of alternating peppers.

3 Seal and cover the terrine with 2 overlapping pieces of plastic wrap. Place the 7-1/2 inch springform pan bottom on the surface of the terrine and weight it with a large canned good. Refrigerate the terrine overnight. Invert, unmold and serve.

Eggplants are in season during August and September.

Eggplant parmesan

Double breading (flour and bread crumbs) creates a crisp coat for eggplants. Baking the eggplant slices, rather than frying them, reduces the quantity of oil used in the recipe.

serves 8

2 pounds globe eggplants, in 1/4-inch thick rounds
1 teaspoon salt
1 cup flour
1 teaspoon pepper
4 lightly beaten eggs
3 cups of bread crumbs seasoned with salt and pepper
3 ounces grated parmesan
6 tablespoons olive oil
5 cups tomato-basil sauce
12 ounces mozzarella
1/4 cup fresh basil

1 Toss the eggplant rounds in 1 teaspoon of salt. Drain in a colander for 45 minutes and pat dry.

Preheat oven to 425 degrees

2 Mix the flour and 1 teaspoon pepper in a bag. Place the eggs in a shallow dish. Combine the bread crumbs with 2 ounces of parmesan. Bread the eggplant pieces: flour, egg, and finally bread crumbs.

3 Run the 6 tablespoons of oil over 2 baking sheets. Arrange the eggplant in single layers on each sheet. Bake, rotating the sheets and turning the eggplant until they are a uniform golden brown, 20 minutes. Lower the oven temperature to 350 degrees for another 15 minutes.

Assembly
Spread 2 cups of tomato sauce in a 9x13-inch baking dish. Layer in half the eggplant rounds, overlapping them to fit the pan. Follow by layering with 1 cup of tomato sauce, half the mozzarella, the remaining eggplant, 2 cups of sauce, the remaining mozzarella and 1 ounce of parmesan. Bake 15 minutes and cool 10 minutes. Garnish with basil.

Modern eggplants are no longer bitter, so salting isn't required to expel their bitter juices, only to dehydrate.

Beulah, peel me a grape.

Mae West, *I'm No Angel*

Until recently, grapes were not known for their nutritional benefits. They were thought to be mostly water with little fibre and minimal amounts of vitamins and minerals. However, now researchers have identified a phytochemical found primarily in the skin of grapes that provides a host of healthful properties, including protection against heart disease and cancer. This phytochemical is believed to be a major factor in the "French paradox" - how the French are able to consume high-fat diets along with their daily intake of grape products and still maintain a low rate of heart disease.

NEW YORK STEAKS WITH RED WINE SAUCE

Pan-made sauces are quick and have few ingredients. These sauces look and taste as rich as the labour-intensive classic versions.

serves 4

1 small chopped carrot
2 tablespoons chopped shallots
2 chopped mushrooms
1 bay leaf
3 sprigs parsley
3 sprigs thyme
1/2 teaspoon peppercorns
2 cups fruity red wine
2 cups beef stock
1 tablespoon softened butter
1 tablespoon flour
4 boneless 8-ounce New York steaks, patted dry
2 tablespoons vegetable oil
salt and pepper

1 For the red wine sauce, combine the wine, vegetables and herbs in a saucepan. Reduce the wine at a simmer by half, 20 minutes. Add the stock and reduce by half again. Strain the sauce into a bowl, discarding the spent vegetables and herbs. Transfer the sauce back to the saucepan and return to a simmer. Make a paste with butter and flour and whisk into the sauce and season and keep warm.

2 Heat the oil in a large fry pan fry pan over high heat until it reaches smoke point. Place the seasoned steaks in the pan, leaving 1/4-inch spaces between them. Reduce the heat to medium and brown 4 minutes. Flip and continue searing the steaks another 4 minutes for rare, 5 minutes for medium-rare and 6 minutes for medium. Rest the steaks for 5 minutes before service.

3. Plate the steaks with their sauce, passing the extra sauce at the table.

Accompany
Roasted garlic mashed potatoes

It is important to maintain a simmer while reducing the stock and wine in order to retain the round, fruity flavour of the wine.

PANFORTE

'Panforte' means 'strong bread' in Italian and is a Tuscan Christmas cake. A wrapped piece of the cake is used in a Christmas game similar to shuffleboard. The one who throws the cake the furthest without letting it fall from the table keeps the cake.

makes one 8x8-inch cake

6 ounces dried figs
5 ounces raisins
5 ounces sultana raisins
1 teaspoon orange zest
1 teaspoon lemon zest
1/2 cup flour
1/4 cup cocoa
pinch white pepper
pinch of mace
3/4 cup honey
1/2 cup sugar
juice of 1 orange
1/2 pound toasted, whole blanched almonds
1/2 pound toasted, whole shelled hazelnuts
icing sugar

Preheat oven to 325 degrees

1 Finely chop the figs, raisins and sultanas and blend in the zests.

2 Sift the flour with the cocoa and spices, and toss with the fruits in a large bowl.

3 Heat the honey, sugar and orange juice to melt. Combine with the fruit mixture, almonds and hazelnuts. The batter will be stiff.

4 Line an 8x8-inch pan with buttered parchment paper. Spoon in the batter and smooth with an offset spatula. Bake for 50 to 55 minutes. Cool, dust with icing sugar and slice into 1x1-inch squares.

Panforte companions well with mature soft cheeses.

GRAPE ICE CREAM

The vodka in this ice cream does battle with the frozen custard, maintaining a melt even in the freezer.

serves 4

1 1/2 cups unsweetened white grape juice
1 cup milk
1 cup whipping cream
4 egg yolks
1/2 cup sugar
6 tablespoons vodka

1 Reduce the grape juice in a non-reactive saucepan to 2/3 of a cup.

2 Combine the milk and cream and bring to a rolling simmer. Cream the yolks and sugar in a large bowl. Whisking, gradually add the hot milk to the egg mixture. Cook the mixture in a saucepan without boiling until it coats the back of a wooden spoon. If the custard begins to curdle, cool with an ice cube. Chill the custard at least 3 hours.

3 Blend the juice reduction and the vodka into the custard, and freeze in an ice cream maker according to the manufacturer's instructions.*

Accompany
Chocolate wafers

* It is possible to make ice cream without the benefit of a machine by freezing the custard and stirring the mixture every half of an hour, but large ice crystals will form in the ice cream.

Since homemade ice creams are made without stabilizers and/or preservatives, they have short shelf lives. This provides a good reason to eat ice cream on the day it is made.

Of all the fish in the sea, herring is king.

James Howell, *Proverbs*, 17th Century

According to the National Geographic News, herring may break wind to communicate. British and Canadian scientists have discovered that herring create an underwater noise by farting. The researchers suspect the fish hear the bubbles as they are expelled, helping them to form protective shoals at night. The study's findings reveal that both Atlantic and Pacific herring issue high-frequency sounds by releasing air from their anuses. The marine biologists have named the phenomenon Fast Repetitive Tick, making for the acronym FRT. Unlike the human version, FRTs are thought to bring the little fish closer together.

IRISH WHISKEY SMOKED HERRING

Smoked herring (kippers) under flame is one of the most divine scents in the kitchen.

makes 2 cups

2 smoked smoked herring
2 teaspoons unsalted butter
2 ounces Irish whiskey
1 tablespoon chopped parsley

Preheat oven to 450 degrees

1 Lay the kippers flat, skin side up in a deep flame-proof dish. Dot with butter and warm for 15 minutes. Remove from the oven, douse with whiskey and flambé.

2 Remove the skin from the herring fillets and flake the fish into a bowl accompanied by the whiskey sauce. Serve as a canapé with whole wheat crackers.

Kippered herring are salted and cold-smoked. To ease off on the intense flavour of kippered herring, poach them in milk.

HERRING WITH LEMON MUSTARD SAUCE

High-fat herring have a fine, soft texture and robust flavour that are complemented by a strong condiment such as mustard.

serves 2

4 tablespoons flour seasoned with salt and pepper
2 eggs
2 tablespoons milk
1 tablespoon Dijon
1/2 cup bread crumbs
8 herring fillets
3 tablespoons unsalted butter

For the lemon mustard sauce

1/4 cup lemon juice
1/4 cup olive oil
2 teaspoons Dijon
1 teaspoon minced garlic
salt and pepper
2 tablespoons chopped chives

1 Place the seasoned flour in a bag. Beat the eggs, milk and Dijon in a shallow dish. Shake the fillets in the flour, dip in the egg mixture, then dredge in bread crumbs. Sauté in butter over medium heat till golden. Reserve the fillets, keeping them warm.

2 For the sauce, whisk together the lemon juice, oil, Dijon and garlic, and season. Drizzle the sauce over the herring fillets, garnishing with chives.

Fresh herring are available during spring on both the Pacific and Atlantic coasts.

HERRING À LA LYONNAISE

Lyonnaise sauce is a classic French sauce, usually made with white wine, sautéed onions and demiglaze. It is traditionally paired with meats and poultry.

serves 2

8 herring fillets
4 tablespoons flour seasoned with salt and pepper
1/2 cup very thinly sliced red onions
3 tablespoons unsalted butter
2 tablespoons white wine vinegar
2 tablespoons chopped parsley

1 Place the seasoned flour in a bag and shake to coat the fillets. Sauté the herring in 2 tablespoons butter until golden brown. Reserve the fillets, keeping them warm. Soften the onions in the remaining 1 tablespoon of butter, and smother the fillets with the onions.

2 Deglaze the herring pan with vinegar and drizzle over the fish. Garnish with a shower of parsley.

Herring debone easily. Fillet down the centre bone and ease the bone off the fillet.

By this leek, I will horribly revenge.

William Shakespeare, *Henry V*

Leeks are one of the national emblems of Wales, whose citizens wear them on St. David's Day. According to legend, King Cadwallader ordered his Welsh soldiers to identify themselves by wearing the vegetable on their helmets in an ancient battle against the Saxons. The battle took place in a leek field.

LEEK AND WINTER SQUASH SOUP

Leeks, an esteemed and mild member of the lily family, add a base flavour to cuisine not achieved by onions alone.

serves 8

3 pounds butternut squash
4 tablespoons unsalted butter
2 cups chopped leeks, white part only
6 cups chicken stock
1/2 cup whipping cream
salt and white pepper
1/4 cup toasted pumpkin seeds
I teaspoon smoked paprika

Preheat oven to 350 degrees

1 Cut the squash in half by length and lay face down on a parchmen-lined baking sheet. Roast the squash 1 hour. Cool, remove the skins and roughly chop. Meanwhile, prepare the leeks.

2 Melt the butter in a Dutch oven over medium heat and add the leeks. Cook the leeks, stirring for 5 minutes. Add 3 cups of the stock, bring to a boil then simmer uncovered until the leeks are very tender, 40 minutes. Add the roasted squash and the remaining 3 cups of stock, return to the boil then simmer for 10 minutes. Stir in the cream and purée the soup in a blender or food processor and season.

3 Serve piping hot garnished with pumpkin seeds and pinches of paprika.

Accompany
Feather-light biscuits.

For the richest homemade chicken stock, sauté the bones to extract as much flavour as possible.

Rich and Poor Asparagus

During the 16th and 17th centuries in Europe, the aristocracy didn't eat leeks because they were unfashionable and considered 'poor man's asparagus.'

serves 4

8 baby leeks, white part only
2 cups chicken stock
8 trimmed asparagus spears
2 tablespoons unsalted butter
salt and pepper
3 tablespoons parmesan
1 tablespoon balsamic vinegar
2 tablespoons chopped parsley

1 Cover the leeks with the stock and simmer until tender, 8 minutes. Strain off the stock, reserving it for another purpose, and pat the leeks dry. Steam the asparagus 3 minutes until bright green and cool in ice water, and pat dry.

2 Heat the butter in a fry pan till foamy, and lay the leeks and asparagus alternately, side-by-side. Cook over low heat 3 minutes, season, and sprinkle with the parmesan and vinegar. Arrange the leeks and asparagus on 4 plates and shower with the parsley.

To remove sand from leeks, trim the stalks, leaving 3 inches of green. Cut an X in the root end and soak 30 minutes in 10 cups of water mixed with 1 tablespoon of white wine vinegar and rinse.

LEEK NESTS WITH SEARED SCALLOPS

Select large plump sea scallops rather than smaller bay scallops for this sumptuous beginning course.

serves 4

1 1/4 pounds leeks, white part only
3 tablespoons unsalted butter
1 1/4 cups chicken stock
2 pinches saffron
1/2 cup whipping cream

20 sea scallops (about 1 1/2 pounds)
2 tablespoons olive oil
salt and white pepper

1 Julienne the leeks and blanch for 2 minutes, refresh in ice water, drain and pat dry. Sauté the leeks in the butter, add the stock and saffron, and simmer 10 minutes. Add the cream and continue simmering another 5 minutes. Strain out the leeks and reduce the cream to thicken, 5 minutes. Return the julienned leeks to the saffron cream, season and keep warm.

2 Sear the scallops in near smoke-point oil until they are opaque, 2 minutes each side, and season. The scallops should have a 1/4-inch golden crust on each side while remaining translucent in the center.

3 Arrange scallops, 5 per person, on leek nests and serve immediately.

Often recipes call for the white part only of leeks. But remember to use the tough green portion to flavour stocks and broths.

Squeeze my lemon 'til the juice runs down my leg ...

Robert Johnson, *Kind-Hearted Woman*

Lemons haven't always had good press. Their yellow colour was at one time associated with infamy. Catalan priests excommunicated the lemon, claiming that the devil had not succeeded in making it as round and perfect as the orange and that it had come from his hands as a deformed fruit. Virgil on the other hand, attributed it with protective powers against evil spells: "The sour apple with the persistent flavour is an unrivalled remedy when cruel stepmothers have poisoned a drink." Casanova considered the lemon a miraculous aphrodisiac.

LEMON CHICKEN BAKED IN SALT

A surprising dish when brought to the table, a succulent chicken buried in a stark white salt crust.

serves 4

6 pounds coarse salt
8 tablespoons whole fennel
1 tablespoon whole mixed peppercorns
3 tablespoons fresh thyme leaves
5 tablespoons chopped parsley
2 tablespoons roughly chopped garlic
2 beaten eggs
10 juiced and zested lemons
2 tablespoons olive oil
one 4-pound chicken

Preheat oven to 400 degrees

1 Prepare a salt mixture with all the ingredients but the chicken. Now construct a 40-inch square piece of foil, four times thick. Place a third of the salt mixture on the foil, centre the chicken breast side down and pack the remaining salt mixture around the bird. Encase the encrusted chicken securely inside the foil.

2 Bake 2 hours until the juices run clear. Rest for 15 minutes before carefully removing the salt crust and carving the chicken.

The coarse salt acts as a cooking medium and adds little if any saltiness to the dish.

SHAKER LEMON PIE

This version of the Post-Revolutionary American SLP
has a single crust rather than the more typical double.
The beauty of the electric lemon custard is more showy
in an open-faced pie.

serves 8

4 lemons, preferably with few seeds
4 cups sugar
9 beaten eggs
one 11-inch pâte brisée pie shell

For the pâte brisée pie shell

2 1/2 cups flour
1 teaspoon salt
1/2 pound very cold unsalted butter
8 to 9 tablespoons ice water

1 Slice 2 seeded lemons paper-thin using a mandoline. Peel and pith the remaining lemons and slice very thin. Make sure the lemons are free of seeds. Refrigerate the fruit in the sugar overnight in a non-reactive bowl.

2 To make the pâte brisée, cut the butter into the sifted dry ingredients until the mixture resembles coarse crumbs. Add the ice water gradually, working the dough into a disc. Refrigerate 1 hour.

3 Roll the chilled dough out into a 15-inch circle and fit into an 11-inch pie pan, leaving a 1-inch overhang. Tuck the excess dough into the inside of the pan and crimp the edge to seal. Chill the pastry until it's ready to be used.

Preheat oven to 425 degrees

3 Combine the beaten eggs and marinated lemons, pour into the prepared shell, floating some whole slices of lemon on the surface. Bake for 15 minutes at 425 degrees then at 375 degrees for 30 minutes. Cool before serving with chantilly cream (page 134).

Marinating the lemons in sugar removes the fruit's bitterness.

CITRON COEUR À LA CRÈME

Traditionally, porcelain heart-shaped molds are used in the making of this dessert. The molds have tiny holes in the bottom so the whey from the cheese mixture can escape. A cheesecloth-lined form can achieve the same results, but has no heart.

serves 6

12 ounces cottage cheese
8 ounces cream cheese
1/2 cup crème fraîche
1 tablespoon icing sugar
1/2 cup whipped cream

For the citron sauce

1/2 cup lemon juice
1/2 cup sugar
1/2 cup unsalted butter
pinch of salt
3 beaten egg yolks
1/2 teaspoon lemon zest

1 For the coeur à la crème, blend the cheeses, crème fraîche and icing sugar together. Fold in the whipped cream. Either spoon the cheese mixture into a 3 cup porcelain mold lined with cheesecloth or spoon the mixture into an 8 inch ceramic flan pan lined with 5 layers of cheesecloth. Allow the cheesecloth to overhang the edges of the mold. Refrigerate the coeur overnight on a tray.

2 Make the citron sauce by bringing the lemon juice, sugar, butter and pinch of salt to a boil in a non-reactive saucepan. Whisk in the yolks off heat then stir over low heat without boiling to thicken the sauce. Stir in the lemon zest and chill.

3 Unmold the coeur à la crème, remove the cheesecloth and serve with the citron sauce and lace cookies.

To make crème fraîche, combine equal portions of whipping cream and sour cream. Seal tightly in a glass jar and let stand at room temperature for 24 hours and chill.

You look lovely, I would be honoured if you will accompany me to a modestly priced meal at Red Lobster and then a night of romantic movies and board games.

Pick-up line

Before lobsters were extensively harvested, they grew very old and large. For example, one was taken off the coast of Virginia, weighing in at 45 pounds and was 2 1/2 feet long with a crushing claw the size of the fisherman's head. Today, lobsters are sold at 5 years old and weighing 1 to 2 1/2 pounds.

LOBSTER POOR BOY

A Newfoundland poor boy sandwich.

serves 4

1 pound cooked lobster, in 1/2-inch pieces
1/2 cup chopped fennel bulb
1 cup lemon mayonnaise (recipe follows)
1/2 teaspoon chopped fresh tarragon
salt and pepper
4 panini

For the mayonnaise

1 egg at room temperature
1 tablespoon Dijon
1 cup vegetable oil
2 tablespoons lemon juice
1 teaspoon lemon zest
salt and pepper

1 For the mayonnaise, whisk the egg with the Dijon, and gradually add the oil. Add the lemon juice and zest and season. Chill the mayonnaise for 2 hours.

2 Combine the lobster meat with the chopped fennel bulb, 3/4 cup mayonnaise and the tarragon, and season.

3 Toast the halved panini and spread the remaining mayonnaise on them. Divide the lobster mixture between the panini.

Accompany
Cherry tomato salad

Select lobsters by testing their liveliness. The lobster should tuck its tail under it's body when picked up. It should smell good and have black, shiny eyes.

LOBSTER WITH VANILLA BEURRE BLANC

Vanilla enhances a beurre blanc with its pure, spicy, delicate bouquet.

serves 4

For the vanilla beurre blanc

1/4 cup white wine vinegar
1/4 cup lemon juice
1 tablespoon minced shallots
pinch of salt and white pepper
12 ounces chilled unsalted butter, in 24 pieces
2 scraped vanilla beans

two 1 1/4-pound lobsters
1/4 cup coarse salt

1 For the vanilla beurre blanc, reduce the vinegar, lemon juice, shallots and seasonings in a saucepan to 1 1/2 tablespoons, and strain. Over low heat, whisk the butter pieces into the reduction one piece at a time, adding another piece just as the previous piece has melted. The sauce will look like a light hollandaise. Whisk in the vanilla pulp. If the sauce is not being used within 15 minutes, hold it in a thermos until serving it.

2 Bring 1-inch of water and the salt to a boil in a large stock pot fitted with a wire rack. Add the lobsters, cover and return to boiling point. Reduce heat to medium-high and steam for 12-15 minutes. They are ready when a leg comes off easily. Pull apart, crack and cut into bite-size pieces. Serve a claw with half a tail per person with the beurre blanc.

Rely on plain water for steaming lobster. Neither wine, beer, herbs nor other seasonings in the pot will improve the lobster's flavour. It seems nothing can penetrate the exoskeleton of a lobster.

Lobster en chemise with sauce verte

Probably the largest version of seafood or chicken enclosed in parchment and baked. 'En chemise' translates to 'in a shirt'.

serves 4

two 1 1/4-pound lobsters
1/4 cup coarse salt
4 sheets of parchment
vegetable oil

For the sauce verte

1/2 cup vegetable oil
1 tablespoon tarragon vinegar
2 tablespoons Dijon
1 1/2 tablespoon drained miniature capers
2 tablespoons chopped parsley
2 tablespoons chopped basil
1 tablespoon chopped mint
2 ounces minced spinach
1 teaspoon minced garlic
salt and pepper

Preheat oven to 400 degrees

1 Bring 1 inch of water and the salt to a boil in a large stock pot fitted with a wire rack. Add the lobsters, cover, and return to boiling point. Steam for 2 minutes. Cool slightly and wipe clean. Wrap each lobster in 2 sheets of parchment brushed with oil, crimping the edges to enclose the lobsters. Bake 30 minutes. They are ready when a leg comes off easily. Meanwhile, make the sauce verte.

2 For the sauce verte, whisk the oil, vinegar and Dijon together. Add the remaining ingredients, season and refrigerate until needed.

3 Serve the lobsters with their parchment covers open, with lobster crackers and the sauce verte on the side.

Numbing a lobster by freezing it will mimic winter conditions for the crustacean and so provides the answer for humanely dispatching a lobster. A few minutes in the freezer makes for less agony in the pot.

It is said that the only proper place to eat a mango is in the bathtub.

John de Mers, *Dictionary of Famous Quotations*

A Hindi legend tells the story of the mango tree growing from the ashes of the sun princess, who had been incinerated by an evil sorceress. The Emperor fell in love with mango flower and subsequently its fruit. When the mango ripened and fell to the ground, the beautiful sun princess emerged. Thus, the mango has become a symbol of love in India, and a basket of mangos is considered a gesture of friendship.

SPINACH AND MANGO SALAD

I worked at a restaurant called the Metropolitan Diner. This salad is an adaptation of one of the two house salads.

serves 4

8 cups baby spinach
1 cubed crisp red apple
1/2 cup toasted slivered almonds
4 tablespoons mango cubes
4 teaspoons coconut curls

For the mayonnaise

1 egg yolk
2 teaspoons Dijon
1/2 cup vegetable oil
1 tablespoon fruity vinegar
3 tablespoons mango chutney
salt and pepper

1 Toss the apple, almonds and spinach together, set aside.

2 For the mayonnaise, whisk the yolk and Dijon together, gradually add the oil, then whisk in the vinegar, mango chutney and seasonings.

3 Dress the spinach with the mayonnaise, arrange on 4 plates and garnish with mango cubes and coconut curls.

Mangos are highly aromatic, at their best when their scent has a sweet resinous quality and worst when smelling like kerosene.

Mango chicken

An alternate treatment for sweet and sour chicken.

serves 4

four 4-ounce skinless, boneless chicken breasts
3 1/2 cups chicken stock
pinch of salt
1 tablespoon unsalted butter
3 tablespoons roughly chopped onion
1 large pinch cinnamon
1 pinch of saffron
2 teaspoons fresh grated ginger
1 cup mango chutney
1/2 cup whipping cream
1 tablespoon Dijon
salt and pepper

1 In an 8-inch fry pan, bring 3 cups of the stock and a pinch of salt to a simmer. Add the chicken and poach 10 minutes, never allowing the stock to boil. Poach the chicken until it is firm to the touch. Remove the chicken from the stock, wrap it in foil and keep warm in a 250 degree oven.

2 Caramelize the onion in the butter, add the spices and sauté until fragrant. Add the remaining 1/2 cup of stock, the chutney, cream and Dijon. Reduce by a quarter and season. Purée the sauce, leaving it chunky.

3 Serve the poached chicken resting on the sauce with jasmine rice.

Poaching a chicken breast produces the most texturally butter-like bird bar none. The remaining stock is even richer and may be used to strengthen the flavour of an upcoming soup.

WHITE CHOCOLATE AND MANGO MOUSSE

This mousse can act as a filling for a flamboyant dessert involving a dark chocolate bag cast from a paper lunch bag.

serves 6

1 pound white chocolate, in pieces
1/2 cup scalded milk
2 cups whipping cream
4 egg whites
1/2 teaspoon cream of tartar
1 cup mango purée

1 Melt the chocolate over a double boiler. Off the heat, stir in the scalded milk. Chill the mixture for 4 hours.

2 Beat the whipping cream very stiff, fold into the chocolate mixture in 2 lots: the first to loosen the mixture and the second to lighten it.

3 In a separate bowl, beat the egg whites until foamy, add the cream of tartar, and continue beating until the whites reach the soft peak stage. Gently fold into the chocolate mixture.

4 Layer the mousse and the purée in 6 handsome glasses and chill at least 2 hours.

Mango purées may be purchased or even better made by blending mango flesh in a food processor and straining it through a sieve.

Mussels, limpets husband their tenacity In the freezing slither...

Phillip Larkin, *Livings*

There are 3 methods of mussel cultivation. The most ancient, which is still the main method in France, involves fixing poles known as *bouchots,* upright in marine mud flats and growing the mussels on these. The story has often been related of how an Irishman called Walton was shipwrecked in the Bay of l'Aiguillon on the French coast in 1235; how he decided to stay and make a living by trapping seabirds in nets held up by poles; and how his quick Irish wit led him to change vocations when he observed that the poles were soon covered with infant mussels. The second and third methods are park and rope cultivation.

BLUE MUSSEL SALAD

This is a version of my friend Carrie Pollard's recipe for a cool summer salad.

serves 4

4 dozen scrubbed, debearded mussels
2 tablespoons olive oil
2 tablespoons chopped shallots
1/2 cup dry white wine
4 sprigs fresh thyme
8 cups salad greens
salt and pepper
4 tablespoons chopped parsley

For the lemon vinaigrette

1 teaspoon Dijon
1 teaspoon lemon juice
5 tablespoons vegetable oil
salt and pepper

1 In a large pan, sauté the shallots in the olive oil until they become fragrant. Add the wine, thyme, mussels and season. Cover with a close-fitting lid and steam the mussels until they open, 5 to 8 minutes. Discard the cooking liquid and any unopened mussels. The unopened ones died before they were cooked. Cool the mussels quickly in the refrigerator on a flat tray.

2 Make the vinaigrette by whisking the Dijon and lemon juice together and adding the oil drop by drop to emulsify the two liquids, and season.

3 Remove the mussels from their shells and toss gently with the vinaigrette. Check the seasonings and return to the refrigerator at least an hour.

4 Plate the mussels on the greens, garnishing with the parsley and drizzling with the vinaigrette. Serve with crusty bread and cold butter.

For safety, use the thinner, darker, shelled, cultured mussels rather than wild ones. Wild mussels may be exposed to microscopic organisms (red tide), leaving them contaminated even when cooked.

Mussels canadian

A quick, elegant forerunner to a pasta course.

serves 4

4 dozen scrubbed, debearded mussels
2 cups dry white wine
1/2 cup peeled, seeded tomatoes
1/2 cup minced shallots
1/4 teaspoon hot sauce
1/2 cup whipping cream
3/4 cup chopped cilantro
salt and pepper

1 In a 12-inch pan with a close-fitting lid, bring the mussels, wine, tomatoes, shallots, hot sauce, whipping cream and 1/2 cup cilantro to a boil. Steam the mussels 5 to 8 minutes to open. Discard any unopened mussels. They perished before they were cooked.

2 Transfer the shellfish to 4 bowls and reduce the cooking liquid to 2 cups. Check the seasonings, add the remaining 1/4 cup of cilantro, and divide the nectar between the 4 bowls.

The Pacific blue mussels and green-lipped New Zealand mussels are interchangeable flavour-wise. Go local.

Mussel Velouté

A velouté is a roux-based soup thickened and enriched with egg yolks. Veloutés are considered one of the five 'mother sauces' from which almost all classic French sauces are derived.

serves 4

2 pounds scrubbed, debearded mussels
3 roughly chopped shallots
1 sprig lovage
1 bay leaf
2 sprigs parsley
3 sprigs fresh thyme
1 cup dry white wine
2 tablespoons unsalted butter
2 tablespoons flour
2 cups whipping cream
1 cup fish stock
2 beaten egg yolks
salt and white pepper

1 Place the mussels, shallots, herbs and 1/2 the wine in a large covered stockpot, Bring to a boil for 5 to 8 minutes to open the mussels. Discard the unopened ones, as they perished before they were cooked. Strain the nectar through cheesecloth and reserve it. Shuck the mussels, keeping 12 unshucked ones for garnish.

2 Make a roux with the butter and flour. Gradually add the nectar with the remaining 1/2 cup of wine, stirring over medium heat until thickened. Add the cream (reserving 3 tablespoons) and stock and reduce the velouté 5 minutes. Remove from the heat and stir in the yolks blended with the reserved 3 tablespoons of whipping cream. Add the mussels and season. Do not bring the velouté to the boil after the yolks have been added or the soup will curdle.

3 The velouté may be served hot or cold, garnished with the 12 reserved mussels.

Buy mussels with tightly-closed shells and those that snap shut when tapped, signaling that they are alive. If they are heavy, they are full of sand. Smaller mussels are more tender than large ones.

What a wondrous life in this I lead!
Ripe apples drop about my head;
The luscious clusters of the vine
Upon my mouth do crush their wine;
The nectarine, and curious peach
Into my hands themselves do reach;
Stumbling on melons, as I pass,
Ensnared with flowers, I fall on grass.

Andrew Marvell, *The Garden*

Nectarines are a variety of peach with a smooth skin and a flavour so fine that the fruit is named *nectar,* the legendary drink of classical gods. It is a true peach, not a cross between a peach and plum as some have supposed.

Nectarine, bocconcini and mint salad

A quick lunch based on a favourite of Jamie Oliver's.

serves 4

1 tablespoon lemon juice
1 tablespoon olive oil
salt and pepper
4 quartered nectarines
4 regular bocconcini, sliced
8 cups salad greens, including some arugula
4 tablespoons chopped mint

1 Whisk the lemon juice and oil together and season. Toss with the remaining ingredients and serve with red pepper focaccia (page 152).

The delicate, pungent and fragrant ingredients of this salad may be augmented with a garnish of crispy, fried julienne of white onion.

NECTARINE SANDWICHES

A distant cousin to the mille-feuille, Napoléon, or the napolitain.

serves 4

For the cookies

5 tablespoons soft unsalted butter
1 cup sifted icing sugar
1 teaspoon vanilla
1/2 cup flour
1/4 cup cake flour
3 egg whites

For the chantilly cream

1 cup whipping cream
3 tablespoons icing sugar
1/2 teaspoon vanilla

2 sliced nectarines
1 cup raspberry coulis

Preheat oven to 350 degrees

1 For the cookies, begin by brushing two baking sheets with butter. Cream the soft butter with the sugar, add the vanilla and blend in the sifted flours. Beat the egg whites into soft peaks and fold in. Fit a pastry bag with a large plain tip, pipe the batter onto the baking sheets in 1-inch mounds, 3 inches apart. Tap the sheets to flatten the batter. Bake golden brown, 8 to 10 minutes, then cool the cookies on racks.

2 Make the chantilly cream by whipping the cream and folding in the sifted icing sugar and vanilla.

Assembly
Make the napoleons by sandwiching 3 cookies with the chantilly cream and nectarine slices between them. Plate the napoleons like tiny islands surrounded by seas of raspberry coulis.

These basic vanilla cookies double as wafers for ice creams and sorbets.

NECTARINE AND BLUEBERRY PIE

The filling for this pie is cooked briefly on the stove-top so the flavours can be adjusted before the pie goes into the oven.

makes one 9-inch pie

For the pâte brisée

2 1/2 cups flour
1 teaspoon salt
1 teaspoon sugar
1/2 pound very cold unsalted butter
1/4 cup to 1/2 cup ice water

For the filling

2 cups sliced nectarines
3 cups fresh blueberries
3/4 cup sugar
1 1/2 tablespoons flour
1 teaspoon lemon zest
2 teaspoons fresh lemon juice

1 egg mixed with 1 tablespoon cold water
2 tablespoons sugar

1 To make the pâte brisée, combine the sifted dry ingredients and cut in the butter until the mixture resembles coarse crumbs. Add the ice water gradually, working the dough into 2 discs. Refrigerate the dough 1 hour.

2 For the filling, place half the fruit in a saucepan, and add the sugar, flour and lemon zest. Bring the mixture to a soft boil, stirring constantly. Place the cooked fruit in a bowl and add the uncooked fruit. Add lemon juice to taste and cool to room temperature.

Preheat oven to 375 degrees

3 Roll out the first pastry disc into a 13-inch circle and fit into a 9-inch pie plate, allowing the excess dough to overhang by 1 inch. Spoon the filling into the shell. Cover with the second disc rolled into an 11-inch round. Turn the edges under and crimp. Brush with the egg wash made with the egg mixed with water. Slash the upper crust decoratively, dust with sugar and bake 40 to 50 minutes. Allow to cool 30 minutes.

The nature of pie crust demands that it be eaten almost immediately. A pie which has stood around for a couple of hours often has a soggy bottom.

Complacencies of the peignoir, and late

Coffee and oranges in a sunny chair

And the green freedom of a cockatoo

Upon a rug mingle to dissipate

The holy hush of ancient sacrifice.

Wallace Stevens, *Sunday Morning*

Oranges may have long been associated with fertility because this lush evergreen tree can simultaneously produce flowers, fruit and foliage. In Crete, the bride and groom are sprinkled with orange-flower water on their wedding day to make the marriage happy, prosperous and fruitful. In Sardinia, the wedding limousine is usually a cart pulled by oxen with oranges attached to their horns.

BEET AND TANGERINE SALAD

Tangerines are the most common mandarin orange in North America. The oranges were named for the colour of the robes worn by Chinese Mandarin high level civic officials.

serves 4

1/4 cup fresh tangerine juice
2 tablespoons champagne vinegar
1 1/2 teaspoons tangerine zest
6 tablespoons olive oil
salt and pepper
1 pound whole red beets
1 pound whole golden beets
3 peeled, seeded and segmented tangerines
2 tablespoons chopped parsley

1 Whisk together the juice, vinegar, zest, olive oil and seasonings.

2 Steam the beets separately until tender, 45 minutes. Cool, peel and quarter the beets. Place the red beets in one bowl and the golden beets in another and divide the vinaigrette between them. Chill the two bowls for 2 hours. Toss the beets with the parsley.

3 Arrange the beets on 4 plates using the tangerine segments as garnish.

Consider this salad for a Christmas side dish when mandarins are plentiful and at their best.

ORANGE MOLASSES COOKIES

A cake-like, spicy cookie with a signature crunchy sugar crust.

makes 3 dozen cookies

3/4 cup unsalted butter
1 1/2 cups sugar
1/4 cup fancy molasses
1 sightly beaten egg
3 tablespoons orange zest
2 cups flour
2 teaspoon baking soda
1 teaspoon cinnamon
1 teaspoon ginger
1 teaspoon nutmeg
1/2 teaspoon cloves
pinch of nutmeg
1/2 teaspoon salt

Preheat oven to 350 degrees

1 Cream the butter, 1 cup sugar and molasses, and add the egg and zest to blend. Combine with the sifted dry ingredients.

2 Make 3 dozen balls with the dough and roll them in the remaining 1/2 cup of sugar. Flatten the balls slightly.

3 Bake on parchment-lined baking sheets for 12 to 15 minutes. Be careful not to overbake. Cool and eat with espresso.

Oranges are sometimes dyed with food colour, so colour isn't a good indicator of quality. Rather, look for firm, heavy oranges. Blemishes on the skin don't affect flavour or quality.

CANDIED ORANGE PEEL TUMMY BUSTER

My family typically ate so much of this fruit braid that our tummies were busting.

makes 1 large braid

2 cups milk
2 tablespoons dry active yeast
1/3 cup sugar
1/3 cup honey
2 beaten eggs
1/2 cup melted unsalted butter
8 cups bread flour
1 tablespoon cinnamon
1 teaspoon cloves
1 teaspoon nutmeg
1 cup sultana raisins
1 cup candied orange peel
1 cup toasted pecan pieces

1 beaten egg white

1 Heat the milk to lukewarm and foam the yeast with the two sugars, 10 minutes. Beat in the eggs and butter. Briskly stir in 4 cups of the flour, followed by the remaining ingredients. Add the final 4 cups of flour to obtain a dough that is no longer sticky. Do not knead the dough.

2 Turn the dough into a large oiled bowl and let it rise until doubled in volume. Punch down the tummy buster and double again.

3 Form a three-piece braid with the dough and place on a parchment-lined baking sheet. Allow to rise again for 1 hour.

Preheat oven to 350 degrees

4 Brush the bread with the egg white wash and bake for 45 minutes.

Handmade candied orange peel is superior to the commercial variety, which is made from root vegetables. Some good bakeries carry handmade peel.

For whom the bell tolls

Ernest Hemingway

When Christopher Columbus first travelled to the Americas he tasted the natives' food, which was seasoned with dried pepper powder. The flavour was reminiscent of black pepper; he recognized it from what Marco Polo brought back from the Orient during his own travels. Pepper of all types was a valued spice in 16th century Europe, mostly to flavour spoiled, if not rotten, meat. When Columbus brought the chillies back to Europe, he called them "pimientas"(peppers in Spanish) to increase their market value. Bell peppers are actually a member of the chili family but we continue to refer to them as peppers.

Red bell pepper focaccia

I worked at a fine dining restaurant in Vancouver that used bell pepper ends to make its popular house bread.

makes one 10x16-inch flat bread

1 1/3 cups warm water
1 tablespoon active dry yeast
1 teaspoon honey
2 teaspoons salt
1/4 cup olive oil
1 cup minced red bell pepper, squeezed dry
1/4 teaspoon red pepper flakes
4 to 4 1/2 cups flour

For the garnishes

4 tablespoons olive oil
3 tablespoons grated parmesan
1 tablespoon chopped fresh rosemary
1 teaspoon coarse salt
1/2 teaspoon pepper

1 Foam the yeast and honey in the water in a large mixing bowl. Stir in the salt, olive oil, minced bell pepper and bell pepper flakes. Add the flour by the cupful to form a silky, smooth dough. You may need to add the extra 1/2 cup of flour to obtain the right consistency. Cover loosely with plastic wrap in the same lightly oiled bowl. Allow to double in volume, about 1 1/2 hours. Punch down and double again.

Preheat oven to 350 degrees

2 Fit the dough into an oiled 10x16-inch baking sheet with 1/2 inch sides. Scatter the garnishes evenly on the surface of the dough and then using your fingertips, gently poke indentations all over the bread. Let rise another 15 minutes.

3 Bake 20 minutes, rotating the pan in the oven halfway through, being careful not to overbake. Serve warm.

Bell peppers have more vitamin C than oranges of the same weight.

Ricotta Gâteau with Balsamic Red Peppers

Variegated orange and white stripes give this savoury cake a gift-like quality.

serves 8

2 large leeks, white part only, cut into long strips
2 large carrots, shaved into strips
12 ounces leaf spinach, blanched and chopped
6 ounces ricotta
6 ounces grated feta
3 lightly beaten eggs
3 tablespoons grated parmesan
2 tablespoons bread crumbs
1 teaspoon chopped fresh thyme
pepper

For the balsamic peppers (make the day before)

6 roasted red bell peppers, in quarters
2 tablespoons balsamic vinegar
2 tablespoons chopped basil
1 tablespoon olive oil
salt and pepper

Preheat oven to 350 degrees

1 Blanch the leek and carrot strips 3 minutes, cool in an ice bath and pat dry. Line a buttered 1 1/2 quart casserole dish with alternating strips of leek and carrot, in a spoked wheel formation. Overlap the edges of the dish.

2 Blend the ricotta and feta till very smooth, adding the eggs one at a time. Fold in the spinach, parmesan, crumbs, thyme and cracked pepper (no need to use salt as the feta is salty). Pack into the casserole dish and cover the mixture with the overhanging vegetable strips.

3 Cover with foil and bake in a bain marie for 1 1/2 hours. Rest 15 minutes, then carefully invert the casserole dish onto a serving platter, releasing the gâteau.

4 For the balsamic peppers, combine the ingredients and refrigerate at least 24 hours to allow the flavours to develop. Bring to room temperature for service. Use as a bed for the gâteau slices.

The longer balsamic-infused peppers remain in the refrigerator, the richer they become. Make a big batch and store them for up to a week.

Pan-fried halibut with red pepper confit

Confit traditionally refers to goose, duck or pork that has been cooked and sealed in its own fat. Peppers given like treatment are sealed in vegetable oil which acts as a preservative.

serves 4

For the confit of peppers (make 2 days before)

1/2 pound diced red bell peppers
1 cup olive oil
1 sprig fresh thyme
1 bay leaf
1 sprig fresh rosemary
1 teaspoon chopped garlic
salt and pepper

four 6-ounce skinless fillets halibut, patted dry
2 tablespoons olive oil
1 teaspoon chopped rosemary
2 tablespoons thinly sliced garlic
salt and pepper

1 Two days before service, make the confit. Heat the olive oil in a medium-sized sauce pan, add the chopped pepper, and simmer 30 minutes. Off heat, stir in the herbs, garlic and seasoning. Rest in the refrigerator. To serve, reheat the mixture, strain out the pepper confit and set aside. Keep the infused olive oil in the refrigerator for other purposes, such as vinaigrettes.

2 Pan-fry the halibut in a nonstick pan in olive oil until golden brown, 4 minutes per side. Shower with rosemary during the cooking process. Season and plate.

3 Sauté the garlic in the oil remaining in the pan until crispy. Garnish the halibut with the garlic and red pepper confit.

The sweet red pepper is simply a vine-ripened green pepper.

I have eaten

the plums

that were in

the icebox

and which

you were probably

saving

for breakfast

Forgive me

they were delicious

so sweet

and so cold.

William Carlos Williams, *This Is Just to Say*

The common plum originated in the Neolithic Age when two species of plum self-hybridized. The wild offspring, which propagated somewhere in the northern Mediterranean, was cultivated millennia later by the denizens of Damascus, an ancient node on the trading network of the Mediterranean. Sometime in the Middle Ages this Damascus, or Damson plum arrived in England. Likely, the Crusaders of Richard the Lionheart, returning to Britain, brought along the luxuries of the Byzantium including delicacies of the marketplace - dates, olives, peaches and plums, dried or salted to keep on the long journey.

JOLLY JACKIE'S SCONES WITH PLUM JAM

It is advised to eat scones with preserves and Devonshire clotted cream.

makes 12 scones

3 cups flour
2 tablespoons baking powder
1/2 teaspoon salt
1/4 cup sugar
3/4 cup very cold unsalted butter
1 egg
buttermilk (see step 1 on next page)

For the jam

4 cups chopped Italian plums
3 1/2 cups sugar

Preheat oven to 350 degrees

1 Sift the dry ingredients together. Cut in the butter until the mixture resembles coarse crumbs. Beat the egg in a 1-cup measuring cup and add buttermilk until the two liquids measure 9 ounces. Add the wet ingredients to the dry and gather the dough up into a ball. Divide the ball into 2 discs and cut 6 wedges out of each.

2 Bake on a parchment-lined baking sheet until golden brown, 10 to 12 minutes. Serve the scones warm.

3 For the jam, mix the plums and sugar together and let stand 1 hour. Boil, then simmer, stirring frequently and skimming off the foam. Transfer into hot, sterilized jars and seal according to the manufacturer's instructions.

Jolly Jackie's mother passed this scone recipe on to me. Sue emphasized the importance of using two knives to cut the butter into the dry ingredients in order to minimize the influence of hot human hands on the dough. The colder the dough, the flakier the scone.

PLUM UPSIDE-DOWN CAKE

This is a two-stage method cake. It is quicker and nearly foolproof compared to a conventional yellow cake.

one 9-inch cake

12 Damson plums, halved
1 cup sugar

2 eggs at room temperature
4 tablespoons milk at room temperature
1 teaspoon vanilla
3/4 cup + 3 tablespoons sifted cake flour
3/4 cup sugar
1 teaspoon baking powder
pinch of salt
1/2 cup unsalted, softened butter in 8 pieces
1 tablespoon orange zest

1 Arrange the plum halves cut side down in a buttered 9-inch pie plate.

2 Combine the 1 cup of sugar with a 1/3 cup of water and caramelize the sugar to the amber stage. Pour the syrup over the plums.

Preheat oven to 350 degrees

3 Beat the eggs, milk and vanilla together to make 3/4 of a cup, measure out 1/2 cup of the mixture, and set it aside. Combine the flour, sugar, baking powder and salt. Add the butter, one piece at a time until the butter and flour begin to clump together and look sandy. Add the 1/2 cup egg mixture and mix to incorporate on lowest speed. Increase speed to medium-high and beat until light and fluffy, about a minute. Add the remaining 1/4 cup egg mixture in a steady stream. Scrape down the bowl and beat 15 seconds to combine. Fold in the orange zest.

4 Pour the batter over the caramelized plums and bake the cake 25 to 30 minutes until the top is light golden and a toothpick comes out clean. Rest 10 minutes, then invert the cake onto a serving platter.

Damsons are recommended in this cake because the astringency of the fruit plays off the large quantity of sugar used for caramelization.

COUPE AMBASSADRICE

This recipe has been adapted from Alice B. Toklas's Cookbook after a dessert made by her beloved chef Nguyen.

serves 4

4 Japanese black plums, halved
1 cup sugar
1 cup water
8 small scoops raspberry ice cream
4 tablespoons strawberry purée
4 tablespoons kirsch
1 cup whipped cream
4 tablespoons chopped pistachios

1 Make a heavy syrup with the sugar and water by bringing the two to a boil. Reduce to a simmer and poach the plums until tender, 10 minutes. Chill in the syrup.

2 Using one plum per person, arrange the fruit on four plates, filling each cavity with ice cream, strawberry purée and kirsch. Surround with whipped cream rosettes and a tablespoon each of chopped pistachios.

From the same book, a description of dispatching a live carp:
I carefully, deliberately found the base of the carp's vertebral column and plunged the knife in. I let go my grasp to see what had happened. The carp was dead, killed, assassinated, murdered in the first, second and third degree. Limp, I fell into a chair. With my hands unwashed reaching for a cigarette, lighted it and waited for the police to come and take me into custody.

His instinct for power is as primordial as a salmon going upstream to spawn.

Theodore H. White: of Lyndon Johnson

The mechanisms which enable salmon to return to the rivers from which they set out are complex and perhaps not yet fully understood, but amazing effective. This 'magic' feature may help to account for the prominence of salmon in mythology. In Celtic mythology, Fionn Mac Cumhaill gained great knowledge through cooking the salmon of knowledge. Three drops of juice spurted out of the salmon's skin and landed on his thumb. Instinctively Fionn stuck his thumb in his mouth to cool it and found he knew all there is to know in the world. These were the three drops that contained all the knowledge in the world.

BUCKWHEAT BLINI WITH SMOKED SALMON

Blini are pancakes made with yeast, giving them a slightly sour flavour and a feather-light texture.

serves 6

1 1/3 cups flour
1 1/3 cups buckwheat flour
4 teaspoons dry active yeast
1/4 cup sugar
1/2 teaspoon salt
2 3/4 cups milk
1/2 cup unsalted butter, in small pieces
4 beaten eggs
36 pieces cold smoked salmon
1/2 cup sour cream
6 teaspoons chopped chives
cracked black pepper

1 Combine the sifted flours, yeast, sugar and salt. Heat the milk to 115 degrees and add the butter to melt it. Add the eggs, then incorporate the wet ingredients into the dry. Beat the batter well by hand, 5 minutes. Cover the bowl and allow to rise in a warm place until the batter has doubled in volume, 1 to 1 1/2 hours.

2 Preheat a heavy-bottomed 10-inch pan hot enough that a drop of water instantly evaporates from its surface. Coat the pan with a thin film of melted butter. Stir the batter to deflate it and drop about 3 tablespoons of batter to make a 4-inch blini. Turn the pancakes when their surfaces are bubbly and brown the other side. Keep the blini warm in a 150 degree oven.

3 Serve 6 blini per person with a slice of smoked salmon per pancake. Garnish with sour cream, chives and cracked pepper. Roll the blini into fat cigars and eat by hand.

Cold smoked salmon complements the earthy flavour of buckwheat.

GRILLED SALMON WRAPPED IN PEPPERED BACON

Surf, turf and the barbecue.

serves 4

4 salmon steaks, skinned, 1 1/2 inches thick
4 peppered bacon rashers
oil for the grill
6 tablespoons melted, unsalted butter
3 tablespoons lemon juice

1 Cut around the bone at the top of the steaks and remove it. Trim 1 inch off the tail end and toss it to the cat. Wrap each salmon portion in bacon, securing the rashers with wooden skewers.

2 Prepare a charcoal grill and oil it generously. Combine the butter and lemon juice. Brush one side of the steaks with the mixture. Arrange the salmon butter-side down on the grill, cook 5 minutes. Now brush the top-side with the butter, turn and grill until just opaque, another 5 minutes.

3 Remove from the heat and discard the skewers.

Accompany
Roasted potato salad

The flesh behind the head of a salmon has the most flavour.

CRISPY SALMON SUPRÊMES WITH AÏOLI

A suprême traditionally refers to a boneless chicken breast.

serves 4

four 6-ounce wild salmon fillets, pin boned
1 tablespoon olive oil
salt and pepper

For the aïoli

1 egg yolk
1 teaspoon puréed garlic
1/2 cup olive oil
1 teaspoon lemon juice
pinch of salt

1 Score the fillets' skin side with 3 slashes 1/2 inch deep. Brush the salmon with the oil and season.

2 Heat a heavy-bottomed pan to near smoke point and apply a thin layer of olive oil to the pan. Cook the fillets skin-side down for 30 seconds, reduce the heat to medium-high, and brown the fillets without moving them for 5 minutes. Turn and continue cooking until the interiors are no longer translucent, 4 minutes. Plate the fillets and serve with the aïoli.

3 For the aïoli, combine the yolks and garlic and slowly whisk in the olive oil. Add the lemon juice and season. Refrigerate until needed.

Aquaculture is on the increase in North America. Although farmed salmon are raised in the same salt water as their wild relations, their flesh is insipid and flaccid.

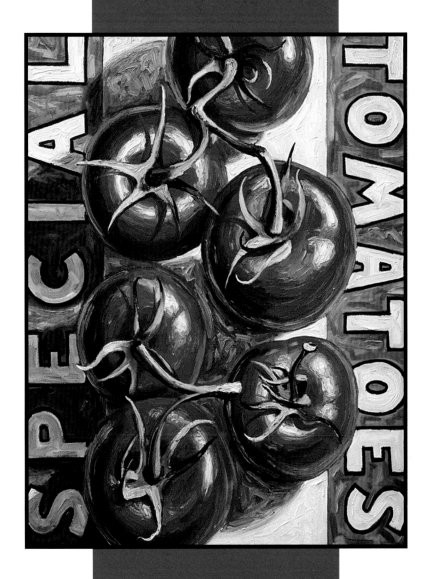

You like potato and I like potahto You like tomato and I like tomahto potato, potahto, tomato, tomahto Let's call the whole thing off.

Ira Gershwin, *Let's Call the Whole Thing Off*

The tomato's Latin name, Solanum lycopersicum, the latter meaning 'wolf peach', reflects the tomato as being inviting yet dangerous, thought to be poisonous. In fact, all parts of the plant except the fruit are toxic. Still, tomato plants became widely cultivated in South America by the time the Spaniards invaded in the 16th century. Although back in Europe it wasn't until two hundred years later that the 'love apple' crossed over from the ornamental to the edible. Today, the ubiquitous tomato must be in thousands of recipes.

BARBECUED DUCK & SWEET CHILI PIZZA

If Naples had patented the pizza, its streets would be paved with gold.

serves 4

For the pizza dough

1 1/2 teaspoons active dry yeast
1/2 cup warm water
1 teaspoon honey
1 1/2 cups flour
1 teaspoon salt
2 teaspoons olive oil

4 ounces very finely julienned Chinese bbq duck
2 tablespoons sweet chili sauce
1/2 cup tomato sauce
3 bocconcini balls, thinly sliced
3 tablespoons grated parmesan

1 For the dough, foam the yeast with the honey in water, 10 minutes. Add the other ingredients and knead to obtain a silky, smooth ball. Allow the dough to rise in a covered, oiled bowl for 1 hour.

Preheat oven to 425 degrees

2 Punch down the dough and roll into a 10-inch circle. Place on a cornmeal-scattered baking sheet. Using your fingertips, make indentations over the surface of the pizza shell. Rest the dough 15 minutes, then bake for 15 minutes, checking half way through to deflate any risen areas.

3 Distribute the sauces over the shell followed by the duck and cheeses. Bake another 10 minutes.

For the crispiest crust, bake the pizza on the lowest rack of your oven.

Hurwitz octopus lasagna

Dave Hurwitz was a commercial crabber in Tofino. Dave's crab traps would sometimes come up containing not only crabs but a well-fed octopus.

serves 8

1 tablespoon olive oil
1 cup minced onion
1 1/2 tablespoons minced garlic
1 pound ground octopus
1/4 cup whipping cream
28 ounces puréed tomatoes
28 ounces drained diced tomatoes
15 ounces ricotta
1 1/4 cups grated parmesan
1/2 cup chopped basil
1 beaten egg
salt and pepper
12 cooked lasagna noodles
1 pound grated whole milk mozzarella

1 Heat the oil in a heavy-bottomed Dutch oven, soften the shallots, add the garlic, and sauté until fragrant. Add the octopus and sauté until cooked through. Stir in the tomatoes and cream, and simmer 10 minutes to blend the flavours. Season, leaving the sauce on the thin side.

2 Combine the ricotta, 1 cup parmesan, basil and egg, season lightly.

Preheat oven to 375 degrees

3 Cover the bottom of a 9x13-inch pan with 1 1/4 cups of the octopus mix. Follow with 3 lasagna noodles, 9 tablespoons of the cheese mixture and 1 cup mozzarella. Cover with 1 1/2 cups octopus mix and repeat the layering pattern, finishing with the remaining sauce, 1 cup mozzarella and a 1/4 cup parmesan.

4 Cover the lasagna with foil and bake 15 minutes. Remove the foil cover and continue baking another 25 minutes until the cheeses are dappled golden. Rest 10 minutes before serving.

Defrost the octopus for 15 minutes before commencing work; grind the semi-frozen octopus with a hand-crank meat grinder.

CHICKEN, TOMATO, SAUSAGE AND LEEK RAGOÛT

A stew similar but not identical to a Louisiana gumbo.

serves 6

1 pound Italian sweet sausages, sliced into 1-inch pieces
3 tablespoons olive oil
1 pound cubed chicken breasts
3 small leeks, white part only in 1-inch pieces
1 tablespoon minced garlic
salt and pepper
1/2 teaspoon hot sauce
4 1/2 cups chicken stock
28 ounces diced tomatoes
1 cored, seeded and diced red pepper

1 Heat the oil in a Dutch oven over medium heat. Add the sausage and brown until golden, remove the sausage and reserve. Sauté the chicken until brown and reserve.

2 Pour off all but 2 tablespoons oil from the Dutch oven. Add the leek and garlic and sauté 5 minutes. Return the meats to the Dutch oven. Add the stock and tomatoes along with the hot sauce and seasonings. Simmer 45 minutes. Add the red pepper and cook another 15 minutes. Remove the meats and vegetables from the Dutch oven and set them aside. Reduce the liquid by one third over high heat. Return the meat element to the pan. Check the seasonings.

3 Serve over rice in shallow bowls.

Choose firm, well-shaped tomatoes that are noticeably fragrant and richly coloured. Keep tomatoes at room temperature. Never refrigerate them as this makes tomatoes pulpy and it will kill their flavour.

Summer's
laugh loud
Of
scarlet ice
A
melon
slice.

José Juan Tablada, *Roots and Wings*

Watermelons have been common in Europe, Asia, the Americas and Africa for so long that early botanists were not sure of the fruit's origins. The question was settled by Dr. David Livingston (of "Dr. Livingston I presume" fame) when he discovered watermelons growing wild in the most remote regions of Africa. Watermelons have been used as canteens on long, water-short journeys; made useful as a potable liquid when water supplies are polluted; and in Naples "the only way to eat, drink and wash your face at the same time".

Virgin Watermelon Daiquiri

To make this drink experienced, add a shot and a half of white rum.

serves 1

1/4 cup deseeded watermelon
2 tablespoons lime juice
1 tablespoon berry sugar
2 cups crushed ice

1 watermelon wedge
sprig lemon balm

1 Freeze an old-fashioned martini glass.

2 Blend the first four ingredients till smooth but not slushy.

3 Pour into the martini glass and garnish with the watermelon wedge and lemon balm.

Cocktails are not dead.

WATERMELON BOMBE CAKE

A watermelon look-alike pool party dessert.

serves 8

2 cups pistachio ice cream
1 cup vanilla ice cream
4 cups watermelon sorbet (recipe follows)
4 chocolate wafers broken to resemble melon seeds
one 6-inch vanilla sponge cake

For the sorbet

1 cup sugar
3 tablespoons watermelon liqueur
3 cups deseeded watermelon purée

1 For the watermelon sorbet, make a sugar syrup by dissolving the sugar in 3/4 cup of water, add the liqueur and chill. Blend the watermelon purée with the syrup and freeze in an ice cream maker according to the manufacturer's instructions.

2 Line a 3-quart 6-inch metal mixing bowl with plastic wrap and freeze 10 minutes.

3 Apply a 1/2 inch layer of pistachio ice cream to the inside of the bowl, refreeze briefly. Cover the pistachio ice cream with a 1/4-inch layer of vanilla ice cream. Fold the broken chocolate wafers into the softened watermelon sorbet and pack into the centre of the bowl. Cap with the sponge cake. Freeze the bombe until it has completely hardened.

4 To remove the bombe from the mold, dip the bowl to the rim in hot water and invert onto a platter. Serve in watermelon-like wedges.

For a low-fat bombe, replace the ice creams with lime sorbet and vanilla ice milk.

WATERMELON WITH CHÈVRE AND SALT

A refreshing introduction to a summer meal.

serves 4

4 wedges of watermelon, rind on
4 ounces chèvre
4 teaspoons olive oil
4 pinches fleur de sel, crushed

1 Crumble the chèvre onto the watermelon wedges, drizzle with olive oil and finish with pinches of fleur de sel.

Test a watermelon's ripeness by checking for its yellow spot. If the fruit lacks the mark, it didn't ripen on the ground. The stem should be slightly sunken and calloused.

INDEX

THANK YOU